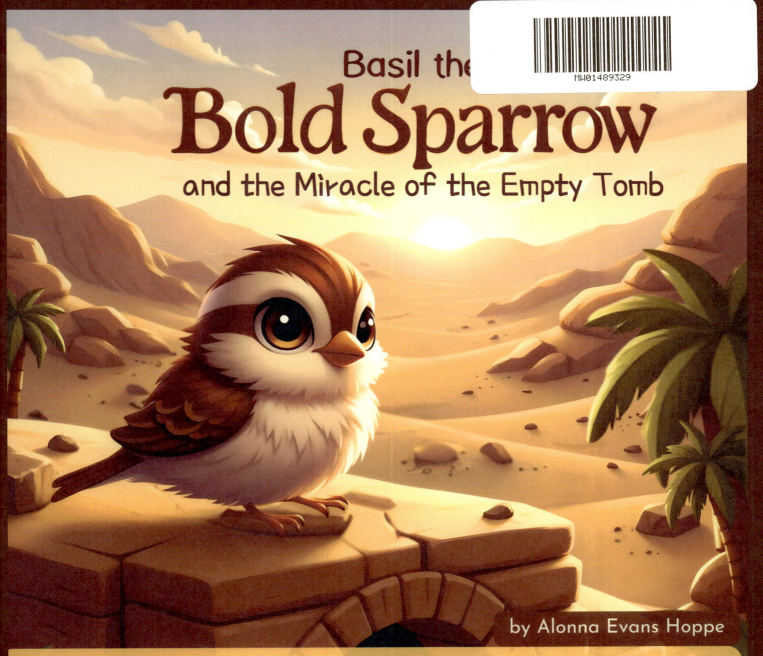

Basil the
Bold Sparrow
and the Miracle of the Empty Tomb

by Alonna Evans Hoppe

A Sparrow's Journey Through the Miracle of Jesus' Resurrection

"For those who seek hope, even in the quietest moments."

Copyright Notice 2025

Illustrations created with AI assistance and edited for a unique storytelling experience
Self-Published via Amazon KDP

Alonna Evans Hoppe 2025

This book belongs to..........

_____

_____

Table of Contents

Scene 1: A City Wrapped in Silence

Perched on a branch outside the city, Basil the Bold Sparrow had seen much in his short life. He had followed Jesus through Jerusalem, watched the crowds, heard the whispers, and seen the sadness settle over the land. But nothing prepared him for what he would discover three days after Jesus was taken away.

Basil fluttered nervously above the quiet streets of Jerusalem. The crowds that had once cheered were now whispering. The city felt different, heavier, like the air before a storm.

"I don't like it," Basil muttered. "Even the wind is holding its breath."

Rufus the Gecko, perched lazily on a warm stone wall, yawned. "You're always flapping about something. What now?"

Tavish the Tortoise sighed from the shade of an olive tree. "Ah, little one. Sometimes things must end before they can begin again."

Basil frowned. "That sounds wise, but also extremely unhelpful."

Scene 2: The Women at the Tomb

At sunrise, Basil saw movement near a rocky tomb.
A group of women walked toward it, carrying jars of oil and spices.
"Ah, now this is curious," Basil chirped. "Where there are secrets, there are answers, and where there are answers, there's Basil."

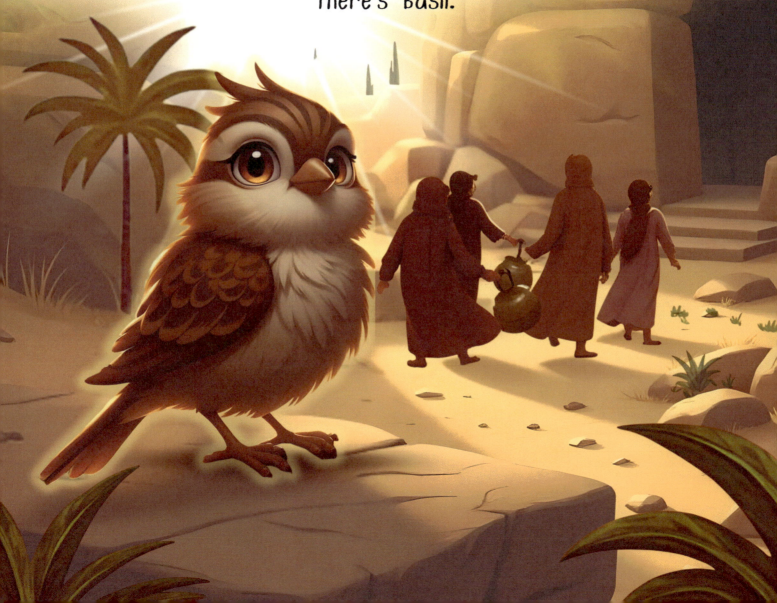

He flitted closer, landing on a branch overlooking the tomb.
But when the women arrived, they gasped.
"The stone—it's rolled away!" one of them cried.

Basil leaned forward. "Well, that's unexpected.
I'd like to file a complaint—large stones are supposed to
stay put."

The women stepped inside, their voices echoing in the empty space. "He is not here! He has risen!"

Basil's wings shot out in shock. "Risen?! As in.not here anymore?! This just got interesting."

Scene 3: The Messenger in White

A dazzling figure in white appeared inside the tomb. "Do not be afraid," the angel said. "Jesus is not here. He has risen, just as He said. Go, tell His followers."

Basil, not usually one for silence,
found himself utterly speechless.

"Rufus," he whispered. "Tell me you're seeing this."

Rufus, clinging to the wall of the tomb, nodded. "Oh, I see it. I just don't believe it."

Basil fluttered down next to Tavish. "Tavish, you're old. Have you ever seen anything like this?"

The tortoise chuckled. "I may be old, but even I know that hope is never truly buried."

Basil took a deep breath. "So, let me get this straight. The person we thought was gone... isn't gone? That's. that's incredible! And also mildly terrifying."

Scene 4: A Journey of Hope

The women hurried away, their faces glowing with joy and disbelief. Basil watched them go, his tiny heart racing.

"We have to follow them!" he chirped. "I need to hear how this ends!"

"Or," Tavish said, eyes twinkling, "perhaps this is only the beginning."

Rufus rolled his eyes. "I think the whole 'end' part is what we just watched happen."

Basil thought about that. "Well, then, I suppose I should stick around to see what happens next. After all, someone has to tell the world."

He spread his wings and soared high above the city, his voice ringing out in song.
And below him, the world was waking up to a brand new hope..

Moral & Message

Even in the darkest moments, hope
is never lost.
Sometimes, what seems like an
ending is actually a new beginning.

Meet the Characters

🐦 Basil the Bold Sparrow – "A feisty, curious sparrow with golden-brown feathers and a big personality. He's small in size but big in heart, always questioning, always observing, and always learning."

🦎 Rufus the Gecko – "A playful, witty gecko with bright green skin and a sharp tongue. He enjoys teasing Basil but is a loyal friend, always ready with a clever remark or a reality check."

🐢 Tavish the Wise Tortoise – "A slow-moving, thoughtful tortoise with a shell as old as time. He carries wisdom from the ages and reminds Basil that patience and perspective are just as important as courage."

👼 The Angel at the Tomb – "A radiant messenger of God, bringing the greatest news ever told: "He is not here. He has risen.""

About the Author

Alonna Evans Hoppe always loved telling stories that bring magic to bedtime.

This is her second book about Basil, but who knows what interesting new adventures await next!

Behind the Illustrations

All illustrations in this book were inspired by the magic of childhood imagination and created using a combination of AI tools and hand-drawn enhancements.

Contact us!

It is important for us to let you know that we appreciate any feedback on our creation and if you have any suggestions for improvement, you can contact us at our email address:

alonnaevanshoppe@gmail.com

Did you enjoy Basil's new adventure? Your reviews help bring more bedtime stories to life!

With deep appreciation,

Alonna Evans Hoppe

Made in the USA
Columbia, SC
10 April 2025

56448536R00020